MW01252538

JOHN MILNE

The Queen of Death

HEINEMANN

INTERMEDIATE LEVEL

Series Editor: John Milne

The Heinemann Guided Readers provide a choice of enjoyable reading material for learners of English. The series is published at five levels – Starter, Beginner, Elementary, Intermediate and Upper. At **Intermediate Level**, the control of content and language has the following main features:

Information Control
Information which is vital to the understanding of the story is presented in an easily assimilated manner and is repeated when necessary. Difficult allusion and metaphor are avoided and cultural backgrounds are made explicit.

Structure Control
Most of the structures used in the Readers will be familiar to students who have completed an elementary course of English. Other grammatical features may occur, but their use is made clear through context and reinforcement. This ensures that the reading, as well as being enjoyable, provides a continual learning situation for the students. Sentences are limited in most cases to a maximum of three clauses and within sentences there is a balanced use of adverbial and adjectival phrases. Great care is taken with pronoun reference.

Vocabulary Control
There is a basic vocabulary of approximately 1,600 words. Help is given to the students in the form of illustrations, which are closely related to the text.

Glossary
Some difficult words and phrases in this book are important for understanding the story. Some of these words are explained in the story, some are shown in the pictures, and others are marked with a number like this . . .[3] Words with a number are explained in the Glossary on page 73.

Contents

Introductory Note

About 4000 years ago, the people who lived on the banks of the River Nile were highly civilised. They lived in cities and built temples where they worshipped their gods. Also, they built tombs and pyramids where they buried their dead. This period of civilisation lasted from around 3000 BC to 500 BC and is known as Ancient Egypt.

The kings and queens of Ancient Egypt believed that after they died they went on a long journey. Their bodies had to be prepared for this journey and many valuable and beautiful things were put in the tombs with their bodies. They believed that they needed these things for a long journey to a New Life.

The bodies of the dead kings and queens were covered with perfumes and oils. Then they were wrapped in cloth. When a body is prepared in this way, it is called a mummy. The bodies were then put into tombs and the tombs were closed tightly. The air could not get into the tombs. A body which is mummified and then sealed in a tomb in this way does not decay. It stays the same for thousands of years in the hot, dry sands of Egypt.

Archeologists study ancient history by digging in the sands for ancient temples and tombs. The archeologists who study the Ancient Egyptian Civilisation search for these tombs so that they can find out more about the way the Egyptians lived. The archeologists study the clothes, the furniture and the food which they find in these tombs. They study the treasures and the writings and drawings on the walls.

But the treasures in the tombs also attract[1] thieves and robbers. In ancient times, thieves often stole the gold and silver which were placed in the tombs with the bodies. The kings and queens were afraid that their tombs would be opened and their valuables stolen. They had their tombs built in secret places deep inside a hill or a mountain.

Today, these tombs still attract robbers. Many people all over the world are ready to pay millions of dollars for the valuables from the tombs. These valuables from ancient times are called antiquities. And there are gangs of international criminals – gangs of thieves from many different countries – who try to steal these antiquities. They then try to smuggle[2] the antiquities out of Egypt and sell them in Western Europe or America.

Egyptian law says that every antiquity which is found must be given to the Egyptian Department of Antiquities. Chief Inspector Salahadin El Nur is Head of a special police department, the Antiquities Protection Department. Salahadin's job is to stop anyone taking an antiquity out of Egypt without permission.

1

Holiday in London

It is hot in Cairo in August – very hot. The people who live in Cairo go away in August if they can. Some go to Alexandria, where it is much cooler, and some of the lucky ones go abroad to Europe or America.

Salahadin El Nur, Chief Inspector in the Egyptian Police, was one of the lucky ones. He was able to go on holiday because no archeologists come to Egypt in August when it is so hot. Archeologists prefer to come to Egypt in the cooler months of winter.

It is hot in Cairo in August, but it is much hotter in the south of Egypt. In the desert around Luxor, the sun can burn a man's body like a bar of red-hot iron. And it is there that most of the archeologists want to work. Many of the ancient temples and cities of Egypt are in and around the modern town of Luxor.

Thursday, 4th August, was Salahadin's last day at work. He was going on holiday for three weeks. His assistant, Inspector Leila Osman, would be in charge while Salahadin was away. At half past eleven, Salahadin tidied up his papers and locked the drawers of his desk. Then he stood up and went over to where Leila was sitting. He gave her the keys.

Leila, like Salahadin, was a graduate of Cairo University. They had both studied Ancient History. Leila was twenty-seven, six years younger than Salahadin. She had joined his department five years ago and was now one of the youngest inspectors in the Egyptian police.

'I'm off to London on Saturday,' Salahadin told Leila. 'I'm staying there for three weeks and I'll be back again on Saturday 27th.'

'And I'll have a holiday here in the office!' replied Leila.

'There'll be nothing for me to do. I'll read the newspapers and count the days until you get back. Don't forget to send me a postcard from Piccadilly.'

'Why Piccadilly?' asked Salahadin.

'People say that Piccadilly is the centre of the criminal world,' was Leila's reply.

Salahadin laughed and hurried out of the office. He wanted to get a taxi before the lunchtime rush hour in Cairo began.

———

On Saturday, Salahadin arrived at Cairo International Airport early in the morning. It was already warm and everyone was getting ready for another day of burning heat. But the passengers were looking forward to going to Europe where it would be much cooler.

The customs and immigration officials[3] knew Salahadin and he quickly passed through into the Departure Lounge. Soon he was in the plane and on his way to London.

In London, everything was very different. It was wet and cold. Salahadin arrived at his hotel in Gower Street just after three o'clock in the afternoon. It was a small hotel, but it was just round the corner from the British Museum. Salahadin was going to spend part of his holiday working in the Museum with a friend, Dr Peter Earl. The British Museum has one of the largest collections of Egyptian antiquities in the world.

On Saturday evening, it was still raining a little, but it was warmer. Salahadin went for a walk through the streets of Central London. He walked down Tottenham Court Road to Leicester Square and then along to Piccadilly. When he was in Piccadilly, he remembered Leila's postcard.

I'll buy it now while I remember, thought Salahadin. He walked into a tourist shop selling postcards and books. Salahadin walked past the bookshelves to find a postcard. He found one which was a photograph of "Piccadilly By Night". He walked back to the counter to pay for it. On his way back, he had a quick look at the books on the shelves. He noticed a book which interested him. The title of the book was *The Mystery of Queen Axtarte* and the name of the author was Dr John Farrow.

Salahadin knew that Queen Axtarte was a queen in Ancient Egypt. And Salahadin had read many books on Ancient Egypt written by famous archeologists. But he had never heard of an archeologist called Dr Farrow.

Salahadin decided to buy the book and read it later. He paid for the postcard and the book and walked out into the busy streets of Piccadilly. It was now raining heavily. Salahadin walked towards Leicester Square. He noticed that a new film was being shown in one of the cinemas. Salahadin decided that was the best way to spend a wet evening in London. He had a meal in a small restaurant and went into the cinema.

It was very late when Salahadin got back to his hotel. He went to bed and soon fell asleep. *The Mystery of Queen Axtarte* lay on the table beside his bed. It was still wrapped up in the paper from the bookshop.

2

Who is Dr Farrow?

W hen Salahadin was having breakfast the next morning, he was called to the telephone. It was his friend, Dr Earl.

'Welcome back to London,' said Dr Earl. 'My wife and I want to know if you'd like to lunch with us today?'

'Yes, I'd like that. Thanks very much. I'll get a train from Waterloo and I'll be at your house by twelve.'

Peter Earl lived in Richmond, a suburb[4] of London. Salahadin knew it well – he had been there many times before.

After breakfast, Salahadin had some time to wait before starting out on his journey to Richmond.

He remembered the book he had bought the night before. He unwrapped it and read what was written on the back cover.

Salahadin started to read the book, but soon it was time to leave for his train to Richmond.

THE MYSTERY OF
QUEEN AXTARTE

Dr John Farrow

Dr Farrow's research provides new answers to some of the many questions about Queen Axtarte. These questions have puzzled archeologists for many years:

▲ **Who was Queen Axtarte?**
▲ **What was the Curse of Queen Axtarte?**
▲ **Why was she called the Queen of Death?**

Dr Farrow also gives his answer to the most important question:

▲ **Where was Queen Axtarte buried?**

In Dr Peter Earl's sitting-room, Salahadin looked out across the street to the Richmond park. He watched an old man with his dog.

'An Englishman and his dog,' said Salahadin. 'I've never been able to understand the English and their love of dogs.'

'And you Egyptians, my friend,' replied Peter Earl, 'what about your cats? Your ancestors[5] – the Ancient Egyptians – loved cats, didn't they?'

They both laughed.

'Talking of Ancient Egyptians reminds me of something,' said Salahadin. 'I found a new book in a bookshop in Piccadilly last night. It's written by a man called Farrow - Dr John Farrow. Have you heard of him?'

'Dr John Farrow – now that is strange. I was going to ask you about him. Have you read this morning's papers?'

Peter Earl handed Salahadin a copy of *The Sunday Times*.

'There's a report on page three that puzzles me,' went on Peter Earl.

Salahadin opened the paper at page three and found the report near the bottom of the page.

The Tomb of the Queen of Death

Dr John Farrow, the young archeologist who claims to have discovered the secret burial place of Queen Axtarte – flew with his wife to Cairo last Thursday.

Dr Farrow has studied the writing on an ancient stone pillar kept in the British Museum. The pillar was brought to Britain many years ago. It was found in the ancient temple of Karnak, which is a few kilometres north of Luxor in Upper Egypt.

Dr Farrow believes that the writing was made by someone who was at Queen Axtarte's burial. That person lived for only a few hours after the burial, but lived long enough to write down where she was buried. Dr Farrow is going to Luxor to find the tomb and to prove that his claims are correct.

'This pillar from the Temple of Karnak . . .' Salahadin began. 'Is there really such a pillar in the Museum?'

'Yes, there is. And it's got some marks on it which might be writing. But no one is certain.'

'It seems that Dr John Farrow is certain,' said Salahadin. 'Who is Dr Farrow? Why haven't I heard his name before?'

Peter Earl told Salahadin what he knew about Dr Farrow.

'Farrow is about twenty-eight years old. He was a brilliant student at Cambridge. One of the best there has ever been. But after he got his doctorate, he changed completely. He left Cambridge about three years ago and went to live with some friends in Wales. He didn't write any letters. He didn't tell anyone about his visits to the British Museum and his interest in the pillar from Karnak. He has written this book and now he has gone off to Cairo.'

'And his wife has gone with him,' said Salahadin.

'I didn't even know that he was married,' said Peter Earl.

'And he's never been to Egypt before,' went on Salahadin. 'He doesn't know how hot it is. It's too hot to search for a tomb near Luxor at this time of the year.'

'Yes, he's not going to find it easy.'

'Who else knows about the writing on this pillar?' asked Salahadin.

'The man who knows most about it is your friend, Professor Gomouchian. And he's in Cairo.'

'Perhaps I ought to be in Cairo too,' said Salahadin slowly and thoughtfully. 'Many people would like to know where the tomb of Queen Axtarte is. And I'm not speaking about scholars[6] and archeologists. I'm thinking of smugglers like the Amsterdam Ring.'

'Yes, you could be right,' Peter Earl agreed. 'The Amsterdam Ring would like to know where the Queen of Death is buried. The treasure in her tomb will be worth millions of pounds.'

'And here is a report in *The Sunday Times*, where everyone can read about it,' said Salahadin.

The two men sat silently for a few moments.

'I'll be late coming to the Museum tomorrow,' said Salahadin. 'I'll have to go to our Embassy and get in touch with my assistant, Leila Osman.'

3

Salahadin is Suspicious

Early next morning, Salahadin was at the doors of the Egyptian Embassy in London. It was not long before he had sent off a telex[7] to the Ministry of the Interior[8] in Cairo and another telex to his assistant, Leila Osman.

The first telex was to his friend, Chief Inspector Ahmed Abbas. Salahadin had worked with Inspector Ahmed before.

The telex said:

```
  IX M .IN  UN
 23 .0  G EM  a

VIA ITT 8.8. 9

ATTENTION: INSPECTOR AHMED ABBAS
           MINISTRY OF INTERIOR/CAIRO

DR JOHN FARROW AND WIFE REPORTED ARRIVING IN CAIRO
LAST THURSDAY. PLEASE CONFIRM ARRIVAL AND INFORM
ME NAME OF THEIR HOTEL.

           SALAHADIN EL NUR
           EGYPTIAN EMBASSY/LONDON

 3X50 EC F  G
 3  X MIN  T  N
```

The second telex, to Leila Osman, said:

```
 AYX A TE  UN
 2 50 EC EM  G

VIA ITT 8.8.79

ATTENTION: INSPECTOR LEILA OSMAN
           ANTIQUITIES PROTECTION DEPARTMENT/CAIRO

DR JOHN FARROW (ARCHEOLOGIST) REPORTED ARRIVING IN
CAIRO LAST THURSDAY. PLEASE INFORM ME OF HIS PLANS
AND MOVEMENTS.

           SALAHADIN EL NUR
           EGYPTIAN EMBASSY/LONDON

 2    EC F  G
  XX A TEC UN
```

Then Salahadin went to the Visa Section[9] of the Embassy and looked at the Visa Applications. He soon found Farrow's application. Salahadin noticed a number of unusual things about the application.

Now this is interesting, thought Salahadin. He has left out his doctorate and he says he's a school teacher. Very strange. And why does he say he's going to Egypt as a tourist?

Salahadin realised that Leila would know nothing about Dr Farrow. Farrow had not written on his visa application that he was an archeologist. His arrival in Cairo would not be reported to Salahadin's office.

———

The replies to his telex messages came in shortly after each other. Leila's telex confirmed[10] what Salahadin had already guessed.

Good, thought Salahadin. She has got in touch immediately with Inspector Ahmed.

```
23VEJ ECYEM G
P4XX APTEC UN

8.8.73

ATTENTION: SALAHADIN EL NUR
           EGYPTIAN EMBASSY/LONDON

NO ONE CALLED DR JOHN FARROW HAS REPORTED TO THIS
OFFICE. NOTHING KNOWN OF HIS MOVEMENTS OR PLANS.
HAVE REPORTED MATTER TO INSPECTOR AHMED.

        LEILA OSMAN

4XX APTEC UN
2.50 LCYEM G
```

CONSULATE GENERAL - THE ARAB REPUBLIC OF EGYPT

(SURNAME in block letters)
NAME (in full) ___MR JOHN FARROW___
NAME OF THE FATHER ___Mr. Charles Farrow___
DATE & PLACE OF BIRTH ___21 September, 1951, Manchester, England___
NATIONALITY ___British___
PASSPORT NO. ___X00783___ DATE OF EXPIRY ___31 May 1972___
DATE AND PLACE OF PASSPORT ISSUE ___Liverpool, England___
BUSINESS OR PROFESSION ___Schoolteacher___
NAME & ADDRESS & TEL. NO. OF EMPLOYER ___Wentworth Secondary___
___School, Newport, Wales 055 09 8525___
PRESENT ADDRESS ___Hill Farm, Langrove, Gwent, Wales.___
TELEPHONE NUMBER ___089 31 5M___
TOURIST/BUSINESS/GRATIS   ONE JOURNEY/MULTIPLE
APPROXIMATE DATE OF ARRIVAL IN THE A.R. OF EGYPT
___4 Aug 1971___ DURATION OF STAY IN THE A.R. OF
EGYPT ___4 weeks___ SIGNATURE ___John Farrow___
DATE ___9 July 1974___

For official use only
TOURIST/BUSINESS/TRANSIT/GRATIS
DURATION ___4___ WEEKS/MONTHS
DATE ___14 July 1974___
FEE ___£ 2.50___

Salahadin found Farrow's visa application.

15

The telex from Inspector Ahmed confirmed Salahadin's suspicions.

```
?5?30 E??.?M G
2?7X M??1?7 UN

8.8.79

ATTENTION: SALAHADIN EL NUR
           EGYPTIAN EMBASSY/LONDON

CONFIRM ARRIVAL OF MR JOHN FARROW AND HIS WIFE AS
TOURISTS IN EGYPT. FARROW'S OCCUPATION GIVEN ON
IMMIGRATION FORM AS SCHOOL TEACHER. FARROW AND
WIFE STAYED ONE NIGHT - THURSDAY 4TH AUGUST HOTEL
MIRABEL. LEFT FRIDAY MORNING. NO KNOWLEDGE OF
WHERE THEY ARE NOW. TRYING TO FIND THEM. PLEASE
EXPLAIN YOUR INTEREST IN FARROW.

          AHMED ABBAS

3?7X M?N?NT UN
23X50 E?YEM G
```

It was two o'clock when Salahadin received the telex messages. It was too late to get a plane for Cairo that day. Also, Salahadin had some things to do in London. He wanted to find out as much as he could about Dr John Farrow from Peter Earl. And he wanted to know if Interpol – the International Police – had anything about the man on their files.

First, Salahadin booked a flight to Cairo for the following day. Then he sent off two further telex messages.

44·X APTEC UN
23·.JJ EG·.EN G

VIA ITT 8.8.79

ATTENTION: INSPECTOR LEILA OSMAN
            ANTIQUITIES PROTECTION DEPARTMENT/CAIRO

RETURNING CAIRO IMMEDIATELY. URGENT YOU MEET ME AT
CAIRO AIRPORT TOMORROW - TUESDAY 9TH - FLIGHT MEA
435 FROM LONDON ARRIVING CAIRO 20.45.

            SALAHADIN EL NUR

23X·· EG·.EN G
4·X·APTEC UN

C·T·. MININT UN
·.X59 EGYEM G

VIA ITT 8.8.79

ATTENTION: INSPECTOR AHMED ABBAS
            MINISTRY OF INTERIOR/CAIRO

ARRIVING CAIRO TOMORROW TUESDAY 9TH - FLIGHT MEA
435 FROM LONDON ARRIVING CAIRO 20.45. URGENT YOU
MEET ME. URGENT - REPEAT - URGENT YOU FIND
FARROW AND WIFE. WILL EXPLAIN WHEN WE MEET.

            SALAHADIN EL NUR

·3X59 GYEM G
3·X·MININT UN

Salahadin thanked the officials in the Embassy and hurried out to get a taxi to the British Museum. As he sat in the taxi, Salahadin asked himself over and over again: Why had Farrow tried to deceive[11] the Egyption officials by saying that he was a teacher and not an archeologist? And why had he said that he was in Egypt as a tourist? Farrow had written all these things in his visa application four weeks ago. But then he had told someone that he was going to Egypt to find the tomb of Queen Axtarte. He had told someone about this, because it had been reported in *The Sunday Times*.

———

Peter Earl had also been busy that morning. He had phoned up everyone who knew Dr Farrow. Everybody said that Farrow had left Cambridge and gone to live with some friends in Wales. But nobody seemed to know anything more. Someone had heard that Farrow was using drugs[12]. Another had heard that Farrow had been in trouble with the police. But no one knew anything for certain.

Finally Peter Earl phoned up *The Sunday Times* and spoke to the reporter who had written about Farrow going to Cairo.

When Salahadin arrived at the British Museum, Peter told him about the calls he had made to Farrow's friends.

'I'm interested in the remark about drugs,' said Salahadin. 'The people who sell drugs in England often smuggle them from the Middle East. And the people who smuggle drugs sometimes smuggle antiquities. Perhaps Farrow is involved[13] with a gang of smugglers.'

'You'd better ask Scotland Yard and Interpol,' suggested Peter Earl. 'They may know something more about Farrow.'

'That's what I'm going to do now,' said Salahadin. 'But first – a question which you can answer – do you believe that Farrow has discovered the burial place of Queen Axtarte?'

'Farrow was a brilliant student at Cambridge. He claims that he has discovered the Queen's burial place. It is possible that he is telling the truth.'

'And other people might agree with you,' said Salahadin. 'If Farrow is involved with a gang of smugglers, he might have told them how to find Queen Axtarte's tomb. I'm sure *they* would be interested in the treasure.'

'But why did Farrow phone up *The Sunday Times*?' Peter Earl asked.

'So that's how the report got in the newspaper,' said Salahadin.

'Yes, Farrow phoned up the paper and told them about his visit to Cairo. If Farrow is working with a gang, why would he do that?'

'Perhaps he is calling for help,' replied Salahadin. 'The smugglers may be making Farrow work with them. Perhaps Farrow doesn't want to help them to find the tomb.'

Salahadin promised to write to Peter and let him know what had happened. Then the two men said goodbye and Salahadin went to Scotland Yard.

―――

Salahadin had arranged to meet Chief Inspector Beaston of Scotland Yard. The Chief Inspector showed Salahadin a file with a short report on Dr John Farrow. Farrow had been fined two years earlier for having a small quantity of cannabis.

'But he never told us where he got the cannabis,' Chief Inspector Beaston told Salahadin. 'If he had told us where he got the drugs, he would not have been fined.'

'What about Interpol?' asked Salahadin. 'Do they know anything about Farrow?'

'Nothing at all,' replied Chief Inspector Beaston. 'As far as we know, this visit to Egypt is the first time he has ever left England.'

'That's strange for an archeologist,' was Salahadin's only remark.

―――

19

It was late when Salahadin got to bed, but he read a little of Farrow's book before he fell asleep. And the next day on the plane he went on reading the book with interest.

I must go and see Professor Gomouchian early tomorrow morning, he thought to himself, as the plane took him across the Mediterranean towards Egypt.

4

The Black Mercedes

Inspector Ahmed and Leila were waiting for Salahadin when his plane landed at Cairo International Airport. They had a police car and a driver with them. The driver set out immediately for the Ministry of the Interior in the centre of Cairo.

'Have you any news of Dr Farrow and his wife?' was Salahadin's first question.

'We have checked every hotel in Cairo,' replied Inspector Ahmed. 'We cannot find them at all.'

'What about Luxor?' asked Salahadin. 'Have you tried to find them in Luxor?'

'Why Luxor?' asked Ahmed.

Salahadin told Ahmed and Leila what he had learnt in London. And he told them about Dr Farrow's book, *The Mystery of Queen Axtarte*.

'In his book,' Salahadin explained, 'Farrow claims that the tomb of Queen Axtarte is near Luxor on the east bank of the Nile.'

'But all the tombs of the Pharoahs and the Queens of Egypt are on the west bank of the Nile,' interrupted Leila.

'Farrow explains that in his book,' replied Salahadin. 'Queen

Axtarte knew that all the tombs were on the west bank. She was a very clever woman and that's why she had her tomb made on the east bank of the Nile.'

'And you think that Farrow has come here to Egypt to look for this tomb?' Inspector Ahmed asked Salahadin.

'I'm sure that's what he is doing,' replied Salahadin. 'And he's not alone.'

'Yes, his wife is with him,' agreed Leila.

'I don't mean his wife,' said Salahadin. 'I think there is a gang of smugglers with him.'

The car stopped at a big roundabout[14] in Heliopolis – a modern suburb of Cairo. A large, black Mercedes drew up beside them.

'Why do you think there's a gang with him?' asked Ahmed.

'I'll answer that question in a few moments,' replied Salahadin. 'First, I want to buy some cigarettes.'

'What do you want cigarettes for?' asked Leila. 'You don't smoke.'

Salahadin did not answer Leila's question. Instead, he spoke to the driver, 'Do you know that cigarette kiosk[15] about two hundred metres on the right?'

The driver nodded his head to show that he understood.

'Stop in front of the kiosk,' Salahadin told the driver.

The car slowed down, moved over to the right and stopped by the pavement. Salahadin got out of the car and walked slowly over to the kiosk. He bought a packet of cigarettes and walked back to the car.

'Don't start yet,' Salahadin told the driver. He turned and spoke to Ahmed and Leila. 'Do you see that black Mercedes parked beside the pavement about twenty metres in front of us?'

They both looked at it carefully.

'It's got a foreign number plate[16],' said Inspector Ahmed.

'That's the one,' said Salahadin. 'Now watch what happens.'

The police car drove away from the side of the road. When

they had driven past the Mercedes, the Mercedes moved away from the pavement and followed them.

'I noticed it earlier,' Salahadin told the others. 'I thought that car was following us. Now I am sure.'

They were approaching a busy road junction in the centre of Heliopolis. There were traffic lights ahead of them and a tram[17] was coming up to the junction from the right. The lights in front of them were changing from green to red.

'Drive as fast as you can,' Salahadin told the driver. 'Get across before that tram comes.'

The driver put his foot on the accelerator[18] and drove across the tramlines. The Mercedes tried to follow behind them. The tram driver rang his warning bell loudly. The tram brakes squealed[19] as the tram tried to stop. But it was too late. The tram hit the back of the Mercedes and the car ran onto the grass. It stopped in the middle of the junction.

'Stop – quick,' shouted Salahadin.

The police driver stopped as quickly as he could. Salahadin, Ahmed and Leila jumped out of the car and ran back. But they were too late. Two men who had been in the car had jumped out. They had disappeared through the crowd of people who were running towards the accident.

'Too late,' said Ahmed. 'They've escaped.'

'Let's have a look inside the Mercedes,' said Salahadin.

Inspector Ahmed went up to a traffic policeman[20] and showed him his identity card[21].

'Go and phone the police at the Ministry of the Interior,' Inspector Ahmed told the traffic policeman. 'Here's the telephone number. Tell them that Chief Inspector Ahmed Abbas is here.'

Ahmed and Leila kept the crowd away from the Mercedes while Salahadin searched through it.

Salahadin sat in the driver's seat of the Mercedes and looked around inside. He picked up a packet of cigars and a book which

Two men who had been in the car had jumped out.

was lying on the back seat of the car. Then he looked in the boot which had sprung open in the crash with the tram. He found nothing else.

Two policemen arrived. Ahmed told them to keep the crowd away from the Mercedes and to wait for the police from the Ministry of the Interior.

'They'll tow[22] the car away with them,' he explained to the policemen.

They walked back again to their own car.

'What did you find?' Leila and Ahmed asked together.

'A packet of cigars,' replied Salahadin. 'Dutch cigars.'

'So it is the Amsterdam Ring,' remarked Leila.

'Perhaps,' replied Salahadin. 'But whoever they are, they're involved with Farrow. Look!'

Salahadin held up the book he had found in the Mercedes. it was *The Mystery of Queen Axtarte* by Dr John Farrow.

5

Professor Gomouchian

Next morning, Salahadin phoned Professor Gomouchian and arranged to see him. He took a taxi to Zamalek, where Professor Gomouchian lived.

Professor Gomouchian lived on the top floor of a high block of flats. Salahadin got out of the lift on the top floor and rang the bell of the flat door. The door was opened by the Professor's housekeeper. The housekeeper knew Salahadin and showed him into the sitting-room. It was an unusual room, full of antiquities – stone pots, vases, and hundreds of small statues[23].

24

The blinds were drawn and it was rather dark in the room. Salahadin looked slowly round.

'Hello,' said a voice. It was Professor Gomouchian.

Professor Gomouchian was an old man – about eighty years old. He had a large head which was covered with long, white hair. He was sitting in a wheelchair[24] and his legs were covered with a rug.

'It's been a long time since I last saw you,' said the Professor, wheeling his chair up to Salahadin. The two men shook hands and Salahadin looked round the room once again.

'You have your own museum here,' said Salahadin. 'It's always a pleasure to come and visit you and look at your collection of antiquities.'

'You don't come here for pleasure,' the Professor replied. 'When you come here, you want to find out something. What is it this time?'

'Have you heard of Dr John Farrow?' asked Salahadin.

'I've got his book here on my shelves,' replied the Professor, pointing to the bookshelves behind him.

'And have you read his ideas about Queen Axtarte and about where she was buried?'

'Yes, I have,' replied Professor Gomouchian. 'And I think he may be right.'

'I'm beginning to believe that he is right too,' said Salahadin.

'We know that Queen Axtarte was afraid of tomb robbers,' continued the Professor. 'It is possible that she had her tomb made on the east bank of the Nile because all the other tombs were on the west bank.'

'But what about all the slaves[25] who dug her tomb?' asked Salahadin. 'And all the nobles[26] who attended her funeral? Why did none of them ever tell the secret of her tomb?'

'The slaves were easy to deal with,' replied Professor Gomouchian. 'The Queen had them all killed.'

'And the nobles?'

'It was the custom to have a feast after a funeral in Ancient Egypt. The great feast after the funeral of Queen Axtarte was held in the Temple of Karnak. Before her death, the Queen ordered all the food to be poisoned[27]. Everyone who attended her funeral had to attend the feast and eat the food. And they all died a terrible death.'

'And that explains the writing on the stone pillar from the Temple of Karnak,' added Salahadin.

'That is a possible explanation,' agreed the Professor. 'One of the mourners[28] managed to write a message on a stone pillar before he died.'

'And the Curse of Queen Axtarte. What do you think about that?' asked Salahadin. 'Do you think she was trying to frighten away any tomb robbers? Or do you think she had another plan?'

Professor Gomouchian wheeled his chair up to the bookshelves and took down a copy of Farrow's book. He opened the book and read out the words which are known as the Curse of Queen Axtarte.

' "I am Queen Axtarte – Queen of Queens. I shall live forever. These are my words: anyone who enters my tomb – anyone who steals from my tomb – anyone who touches my body – that person will die – that person will die a terrible death. And many more shall die with him." '

'If you found the Queen's tomb, would you go into it and touch anything?' Salahadin asked the Professor.

'No, I would not,' was the immediate reply. 'I would want to have a lot of scientific tests done before I did anything at the tomb of Queen Axtarte.'

'But, why?'

The Professor took down another book from his bookshelves. It was called *Poisons and Diseases*[29] *in Ancient Egypt.*

'The Ancient Egyptians knew much more about the world than we think,' he told Salahadin. 'They knew something about disease and about poisons. There were many great plagues in

Ancient Egypt. It is possible that Queen Axtarte had the germs of a terrible disease put in her tomb.'

'So if anyone found the tomb, they might be in great danger?'

'If anyone found the tomb and went inside, they would be in great danger,' replied Professor Gomouchian.

'I must go to Luxor immediately,' said Salahadin. 'Can you show me where the tomb might be?'

The Professor wheeled his chair to where a large map of Ancient Egypt was hanging on the wall. He took up a stick and pointed to a place thirty kilometres north-east of Karnak.

'That's where Farrow says it is,' he said. 'And I agree with him.'

———

While Salahadin was talking to Professor Gomouchian, Leila and Ahmed were at the Hotel Mirabel. They asked to speak to the Manager who was not pleased to see them.

'We've had enough trouble from the police already because of Mr Farrow,' the Manager said. 'There's nothing more we can do to help you.'

'Yes, there is,' Leila said politely. 'We want to see the room that Mr and Mrs Farrow stayed in.'

The Manager checked the hotel register[30].

'Room 501,' the Manager told them. 'It's on the fifth floor – and it's empty. You can look there if you want.'

Room 501 was a small room. It had one window which looked out onto the roof of a block of flats. There was a double bed, a wardrobe, and a small chest of drawers in the room. There was a small bathroom at one side.

Leila searched the bed – the mattress and the pillows. Then

she looked inside the wardrobe and the chest of drawers. Ahmed searched the floor, the walls, and the lightshades. Then he looked carefully through the bathroom. They found nothing.

'There's nothing here,' said Ahmed. 'Let's get out of this room.'

Leila had a last look round, but she found nothing. As she was walking to the door, she stopped at the window and looked out. The roof of a block of flats was quite near the window and slightly below it. The roof was covered with all kinds of rubbish.

'I think we've found something,' said Leila.

Leila had seen a book lying among the rubbish. It was just under the window of room 501. And, from the hotel bedroom window, Leila could read the title of the book. It was *The Mystery of Queen Axtarte*.

6

A Call for Help

Forty minutes later, Leila and Ahmed were back in Salahadin's office near Tahrir Square. Salahadin had arrived a few minutes before them and was speaking on the telephone. He was arranging for a police plane to take him up to Luxor. He had a large map on the desk in front of him. It was a map of Luxor and the desert around Luxor to the north and to the east. Salahadin had marked a large X on the map about thirty kilometres north-east of Karnak.

'OK, one o'clock at Cairo airport,' said Salahadin on the telephone. 'Yes, I'll be there. Tell the pilot to be ready to take off at one o'clock.'

Salahadin put the telephone down and Leila placed Farrow's book on top of the map in front of him.

'We've found another message from Farrow,' she said. 'It's on page ten.'

Salahadin opened the book and turned the pages. Farrow's message on page ten had been written quickly.

'So I was right. The news report in *The Sunday Times* was a message. And it is the Amsterdam Ring. Jan Greer is a well-known criminal. He is wanted by Interpol for smuggling and murder.'

Salahadin stood up. He walked over to a wall which was covered with a large map of Cairo.

'I'm flying up to Luxor at one o'clock,' he said. 'Leila, you and Ahmed will have to find Farrow's wife.'

'Cairo's a big city,' said Leila. 'It won't be easy to find her.'

Salahadin pointed at the map of Cairo.

'Christine Farrow is being held by the Amsterdam Ring – they're all Europeans – and she's English,' he explained. 'They are foreigners here in Egypt. If they are holding the woman in

29

HELP –

My name is Farrow.
I'm a prisoner of a gang of
smugglers. They want me to
take them to the tomb of Queen
Axtarte. My wife held in Cairo by
man called Greer. Gang afraid of
policeman called Salahadin.

PASS THIS MESSAGE TO
POLICEMAN SALAHADIN.

Queen's tomb 30 kilometres
north-east of Karnak between
snake's head and sitting man.

Don't open tomb.

Great danger.

an Arab part of the city, someone would notice them. They must be in a European part of Cairo – somewhere where lots of foreigners live.'

Salahadin placed his finger on the large part of Cairo, called Heliopolis.

'Lots of Europeans live here,' he said. 'They could be in a house or a flat in Heliopolis.'

Salahadin moved his hand to the centre of Cairo. He pointed to Zamalek where Professor Gomouchian lived. 'Or they could be somewhere here.'

'The men who own the small shops in the streets – they will remember if they have seen any strangers,' said Ahmed. 'I'll send my policemen to the European parts of Cairo. They'll ask the shopkeepers if they have noticed any strangers in the last week.'

'And I'll go to the small markets in Heliopolis,' said Leila. 'I'll speak to the servants who go shopping there. One of them may have noticed something unusual.'

Ahmed went back to Salahadin's desk and picked up Farrow's book.

'What does Farrow mean by "great danger"?' he asked.

Salahadin told them about his visit to Professor Gomouchian.

'The explanation is here in Farrow's book,' he replied. 'And Professor Gomouchian agrees that Farrow may be right. It is possible that Queen Axtarte had the germs of a terrible disease put into her tomb. Anyone who goes inside the tomb will die.'

'So if the Amsterdam Gang take anything out of the tomb, they could spread the disease everywhere,' said Leila.

'That's right,' replied Salahadin. 'It's part of the Queen's Curse. "The person who enters my tomb will die a terrible death – and many more shall die with him."'

7

In the Desert

The desert to the east of the River Nile and north of Karnak
is rocky and mountainous. There are many hills and mountains and deep valleys.

There was a lorry in one of these valleys, about twenty
kilometres north-east of Karnak. The lorry was parked beside a
large rock. There were three men in the shade of the rock. They
were keeping out of the heat of the midday sun.

'You've been telling us lies, Farrow,' one man said. He was
tall with a red beard. 'You know where the tomb is, but you're
pretending[31] not to know.'

Farrow looked at the Dutchman.

'I don't know where it is, Keesing,' said Farrow. 'In my book
I say that the Queen's tomb is somewhere near here. But I don't
know where it is exactly.'

De Fries, the other Dutchman, was a small man wearing dark
glasses. He spoke quietly to Keesing.

'Farrow's telling lies,' he said. 'We've been here in this desert
for three days and we have not found the tomb. But I'm sure
Farrow knows where the tomb is.'

'We are wasting time, Farrow,' said Keesing. 'If we don't get
to the tomb this evening, I won't call Greer on the radio. Greer
has his orders. You'll never see your wife again.'

Farrow knew what the orders were. Keesing had a powerful
radio transmitter[32] in the back of the lorry. He spoke to Greer
every evening before seven o'clock. If Greer did not get a call by
seven o'clock, he had orders to get rid of [33] Christine Farrow.

Keesing turned and walked to the lorry. After a few moments,
de Fries spoke to Farrow.

'Greer is a cruel and heartless man.' said de Fries. 'If he does

32

not get a radio call by seven, he will kill your wife. Don't be a fool. Take us to the tomb now.'

'I've told you a hundred times,' shouted Farrow, 'I don't know where the tomb is.'

'It's after midday now,' said de Fries. 'You have until seven o'clock. You know what will happen then. Keesing will not call Greer on the radio. And Greer is a cruel man - a very cruel man.'

Farrow sat in silence. He thought of his wife, Christine. She was young and beautiful. Farrow remembered how happy they had been. It seemed a long time ago. They had met Keesing and de Fries in Wales. That had been the end of their happiness.

'All right, I'll take you there,' Farrow said. 'The tomb is about ten kilometres away, but it won't be easy to get there. We'll have to hurry. And when we find the tomb, I'm going to leave you. I don't want to be near that tomb when it's opened.'

Keesing and de Fries did not say anything. They climbed up into the cab of the lorry and waited for Farrow.

'Remember, Farrow, you've got until seven o'clock,' said Keesing. 'If we don't find this tomb by then, your wife will die.'

De Fries started the engine of the lorry and waited for Farrow to tell him where to go.

'Drive along this valley,' said Farrow. 'At the end of the valley we must turn left and travel north. And we must get up onto higher ground. I want to see where we are.'

De Fries drove carefully and slowly over the rough ground. There were large stones everywhere. The heat of the sun was like a burning fire.

'This heat's terrible,' said Keesing. 'Can't you go any faster?'

'If I go any faster, we'll hit a rock,' replied de Fries. 'Then we'll be stuck here for hours.'

They drove on. When the lorry reached the end of the valley, de Fries stopped. He turned to Farrow.

'Where do we go now?' he asked.

Farrow climbed down from the cab and took out his

compass[34]. He looked at the compass and he looked at the hills around him. Then he climbed back into the lorry.

'Turn to the left here,' Farrow said to de Fries. 'And try to get up that slope in front of us. We'll be able to see around us from the top of the slope.'

The lorry started to climb the steep slope to their left.

'Stop, you fool!' Keesing shouted at de Fries. 'Luxor airport is not far from here. We've seen four planes in the last three days. We've seen them, but we don't want them to see us.'

De Fries stopped the lorry.

'If we don't go up higher, I won't be able to see where we are,' said Farrow.

The men sat in the cab in silence. Keesing turned to Farrow.

'Get out and climb up,' he said. 'The lorry stays down here.'

Farrow started to climb the slope. De Fries turned to Keesing.

'Aren't we going up with him?' he asked.

'He won't run away,' was Keesing's reply. 'He's got no water. He knows he will die in the desert without water. And he knows that his wife will die too.'

Farrow felt dizzy[35] in the heat of the sun. He found shade behind a large rock.

I've got to make them drive the lorry up onto the hill, he thought to himself. Someone may see us from the air and report us to the police. That's my only hope.

'Which way do we take now?' de Fries asked Farrow when he got back.

'There's no way round this hill,' replied Farrow. 'We have to drive up here and over the top of the hill.'

'We should have gone up there with him,' de Fries said to Keesing. 'We don't know if he's telling the truth.'

'If there's no way down the other side,' replied de Fries, 'we'll turn round and head back to Luxor.'

'I don't think he is lying,' said Keesing. 'He knows what will happen to his wife. We'll go up and over the top of the hill.'

8

Dr Jusef Strengel

While de Fries was driving slowly up the slope in the desert, Salahadin was flying south towards Luxor. He was sitting beside the pilot in a police plane. He could see the River Nile below him.

'We're getting near Luxor now,' said the pilot. 'I'll turn east. Then I'll turn south and fly over the desert towards Luxor airport.'

A few minutes later they were flying over the desert. Salahadin looked through the binoculars[36]. He could see the rocks, valleys, and mountains below them.

'It's like a mirror,' he said to the pilot, 'the sun is shining back from the sand and rocks.'

'You'll see more clearly when we get down lower,' the pilot told him.

Salahadin studied the map in front of him for a few moments. Then he looked again through the binoculars at the ground below them.

'We're nearly there,' he said. 'I think the tomb is somewhere down there.'

The plane flew lower. Suddenly Salahadin gave the binoculars to the pilot.

'What can *you* see down there?' he asked.

The pilot took the binoculars and looked down at the desert.

'It's a lorry,' he said to Salahadin. 'It's moving over a high hill.'

'It must be them,' said Salahadin, taking back the binoculars and looking down at the lorry.

'Shall I circle round and go lower?' the pilot asked.

'No – we don't want to make them suspicious. Keep flying towards Luxor airport.'

The plane flew on and Salahadin studied the ground below them through the binoculars.

'Look,' he said after a few moments. 'There's another lorry down there. And its bigger than the first lorry.'

'Is it travelling with the first lorry?' asked the pilot.

'I don't know,' replied Salahadin slowly. 'It's about three kilometres south of the first lorry, but it's travelling in the same direction.'

'That's interesting,' said the pilot. 'If people are together in the desert, they keep close to one another.'

But who could be in this other lorry? said Salahadin to himself.

Salahadin carefully marked the positions of both lorries on the map. The pilot got ready to land at Luxor airport.

Police Inspector Musa Angheli was waiting for Salahadin at Luxor airport. The Inspector had met Salahadin many times. Salahadin had often come to visit the ancient monuments around Luxor. The two men shook hands.

'A telex has just arrived for you from Chief Inspector Ahmed in Cairo,' said Inspector Musa. 'You'd better read the telex in my office in the airport building. It's too hot to stand out here in the sun.'

On their way to the airport building, Salahadin told Musa about the two lorries he had seen in the desert.

'Perhaps this telex will explain why there are two lorries in the desert,' said Inspector Musa.

There was a small fan on the desk in Inspector Musa's office. The fan moved the air around, but it did not make the office cooler. Salahadin sat down and read the telex from Ahmed.

```
77XX LUXAR UN
?!<X MININT UN

10.8.73

ATTENTION: INSPECTOR SALAHADIN EL NUR
           LUXOR AIRPORT

RECEIVED REPORT ON THE BLACK MERCEDES. NO- REPEAT.
NO - FINGERPRINTS OF THE AMSTERDAM RING IN THE
CAR. BUT ONE SET OF PRINTS THOSE OF DR JUSEF
STRENGEL - REPEAT DR JUSEF STRENGEL. NO NEWS YET
OF CHRISTINE FARROW.

       AHMED ABBAS

5!!X MININT PA
77Y. LUXAP UN
```

'So, Dr Jusef Strengel is back in Egypt,' said Salahadin.

'A black Mercedes followed us in Cairo,' Salahadin began. 'Ahmed has found out who owns it. The Mercedes belongs to Dr Strengel.

'We know a lot about Dr Strengel,' Salahadin went on. 'His father was German and his mother was Lebanese. He smuggles antiquities. But he's different from the other smugglers. People like the Amsterdam Ring smuggle antiquities and sell them to make money. Strengel has lots of money of his own. He has one of the largest private collections of Egyptian antiquities in the world. He's not interested in making money – he wants the antiquities for his own collection.'

'And he wants the treasures of Queen Axtarte for his collection,' added Inspector Musa.

'That's right,' replied Salahadin. 'And I'm sure that he's out there in the desert in one of those lorries. I think that the Amsterdam Ring is in the first lorry with Farrow. Farrow is taking them to the tomb and Strengel is following them.'

Salahadin discussed the situation with Inspector Musa. There were now two gangs of smugglers out in the desert. Salahadin and Musa could not fight them by themselves. They would have to have help.

'We have a new Range Rover here,' suggested Musa. 'It's the best kind of vehicle for moving over rocky ground in the desert. And I've got a good driver who knows the desert tracks[37]. We can take three policemen with us.'

Salahadin agreed to Musa's suggestion and soon the Range Rover was ready to leave. The three policemen had rifles[38] with them. Salahadin and Musa had revolvers and there was a box of dynamite[39] in the back. Salahadin got it from a store at the airport.

'What's the dynamite for?' asked Musa.

'We may need it,' replied Salahadin. 'I'll explain why later.'

Salahadin showed the driver the map. He pointed to the place he had marked.

'How long will it take us to get there?' he asked the driver.

'It's very rocky ground out there,' replied the driver. 'If we're lucky, we may get there in three or four hours.'

'Drive as quickly as you can,' said Salahadin.

The driver started the engine and the Range Rover set out into the desert.

9

The House in Heliopolis

Back in Cairo, Ahmed and Leila were searching for Christine Farrow.

Policemen were questioning all the shopkeepers – especially those who sold cigarettes or food in small street shops.

Leila had policewomen working for her. They were visiting the small markets in the parts of Cairo where Europeans lived. The servants who work for the Europeans often shop in these markets in the afternoon.

In a small market in Heliopolis, a new servant began to do her shopping. No one had seen her there before. But servants are always friendly and they smiled at the new servant and spoke to her.

'Be careful of Ismael – he charges too much money for vegetables,' one woman said.

'Count your change carefully at Abdul Rahman's, the butcher's,' said another.

Some women were sitting talking in the shade of a large tree. Leila, the new servant, sat down beside them and listened to their talk.

Most of the conversation was about prices and wages.

Leila sat and listened. She knew that she must not ask the women questions. If she asked them about their work, they would become suspicious and tell her nothing.

After a few minutes, a young woman sat down beside them. One of the women said, 'How are you, today, Fatima? And how's the sick European woman?'

'I think she's still there,' replied Fatima. 'She hasn't been out of the bedroom once. What a wonderful life she has! Her husband does all the work in the house.'

All the women laughed.

'Is she very beautiful?' someone asked.

'I've told you before – I've never seen her,' replied Fatima. 'But she must be very beautiful. He does all the housework and she stays in her bedroom. I'm not allowed in there – the door is always locked. My job is to do the shopping and clean the kitchen – that's all.'

'And you're well paid for it too,' said another woman.

Everybody laughed loudly.

Fatima picked up her shopping basket. 'I must go back now. He'll be waiting for me.'

There was more laughter and Fatima walked way. Leila stood up and said goodbye to the women. She followed Fatima for about ten minutes. Fatima stopped in front of an old house and knocked at the door. A man's face appeared at an upstairs window. Fatima stood waiting at the door.

Someone is being very careful, Leila thought to herself.

A few minutes later, the door opened and Fatima went inside. The door closed immediately.

Leila hurried to a small shop at the end of the street and asked to use the telephone. Half an hour later, Chief Inspector Ahmed arrived with two policemen. They stopped the car where Leila was waiting for them.

Leila told Ahmed about the servant in the market. Then she showed Ahmed the house.

Fatima stopped in front of an old house and knocked at the door.

'Fatima, the servant, says there's a sick European woman in the bedroom,' Leila explained to Ahmed. 'Fatima has never seen the woman and the bedroom door is always locked. Perhaps this is the house we are looking for.'

'But we must make certain,' said Ahmed cautiously[40]. 'It may not be Christine Farrow. Perhaps it is a sick woman.'

'We must make certain,' said Leila. 'I must get inside the house and find out who she is.'

'But how are you going to get inside?' asked Ahmed.

'Let's wait until Fatima comes out. Perhaps she will help us.'

They sat in the car waiting. Just after five o'clock, Fatima came out of the house again. She had a basket in one hand and a bunch of keys in the other. Leila and Ahmed got out of the car. Leila stopped Fatima and spoke to her. She showed Fatima her police identity card. 'We want to ask you about the man you work for,' said Leila.

'He's a foreigner,' replied Fatima.

'And what about the woman in the bedroom?' asked Leila.

'I've never seen her,' replied Fatima. 'The bedroom door is always locked.'

'But if you haven't seen her, how do you know it's a woman in the bedroom?' said Ahmed.

'I've heard her crying – and I know the sound of a woman crying.'

'How long has she been in the bedroom?' Leila asked.

'About five days,' replied Fatima. 'Since last Friday.'

Leila and Ahmed looked at one another.

'Where are you going now?' Leila asked Fatima.

Fatima told them that she was going to buy bread. Because of the heat in Cairo, bread does not stay fresh. In the morning, people buy bread for breakfast and lunch. Then they buy more fresh bread in the evening.

'Are those the keys of the house?' asked Leila.

'The foreigner locks himself in his bedroom every evening

between six and seven,' Fatima explained. 'It's the only time he gives me the keys to the house.'

'What does he do in his bedroom every evening?' asked Ahmed.

'I don't know what he does in there,' replied Fatima. 'But sometimes I've heard voices. But there's no one in there but him.'

'Will you help us?' Leila asked Fatima.

'What's happening?' asked Fatima. 'Who are you? I don't want to get into any trouble.'

'We are police officers,' she explained again. 'You won't get into trouble if you help us.'

'What do you want me to do?' asked Fatima.

'We don't want you to do anything,' replied Leila. 'We want to find out more about the people you work for. Let me take the bread back into the house.'

Fatima was not happy about this suggestion. But finally she agreed.

'I'm worried about this,' said Ahmed when Leila was ready to go into the house. 'It could be very dangerous.'

'It's the easiest way of getting into the house,' said Leila. 'And we must make sure that it is Christine Farrow who is locked in that bedroom.'

'What will you do if it is her?' Ahmed asked.

'That's easy,' replied Leila. 'I'll open the front door and let you in. Make sure you are waiting near the door with the two policemen.'

Leila turned to Fatima, 'Now tell me again,' she said, 'where is his bedroom and where is the bedroom with the woman in it?'

Fatima explained once again and Leila listened carefully.

'Good,' she said. 'I'll remember that easily.'

Leila walked up to the front door with the keys in her hand.

10

The Valley of Death

It was just after five o'clock when Farrow told de Fries to stop the lorry. They were at the entrance to a narrow valley. 'We're here now,' said Farrow. 'The Queen's tomb is in this valley.'

'How do you know?' Keesing asked.

Farrow pointed up at the mountain top to the east.

'That looks like a snake, doesn't it?' he asked.

Keesing and de Fries looked up. The top of the mountain was about three hundred metres long. It ended with a great rock rising high in the sky. The mountain top looked like a snake with its head raised.

45

'And that's a sitting man,' Farrow continued, pointing to the mountain top to the west.

Keesing and de Fries looked upwards towards the setting sun. In the middle of the mountain top there was a large rock. It looked like a man's head. Below the rock, a gully[41] ran down the mountain side to the bottom of the valley. The mountain had the shape of a sitting man.

'A snake with raised head and a sitting man guard the tomb of Queen Axtarte,' said Farrow. 'Those words are written on the pillar from the Temple at Karnak.'

'And where's the tomb?' said Keesing turning to Farrow.

Farrow pointed to the gully that ran up the mountain side.

'Somewhere between the legs of the sitting man,' he told Keesing. 'That's all I know. You'll have to go and look for it.'

They climbed back into the lorry and de Fries drove down the valley to the bottom of the gully.

'You know that it can take a long time to get inside a tomb,' said Farrow.

'Why is that?' asked Keesing.

'The Ancient Egyptians always made secret entrances to the tombs,' replied Farrow. 'And they sealed the entrance with huge rocks. They wanted to keep out tomb robbers. It could take you years to get inside.'

'We've got a box of dynamite in the back of the lorry,' Keesing told Farrow. 'When we find the entrance, it won't take us long to blast[42] our way in.'

'What about the Queen's Curse? Aren't you afraid of that?' asked Farrow.

'That was written a long time ago,' replied Keesing. 'The Queen wanted to frighten tomb robbers. It doesn't mean anything today.'

'You could be wrong, you know,' said Farrow. 'I'm going to

get as far away from you as I can.'

'Don't you want to make sure that I radio to Greer?' asked Keesing.

Farrow did not know what to do. If Keesing did not radio, Greer would Kill Cristine. So Farrow had to stay near.

Farrow looked up the gully. There was a large rock on the right leg of the sitting man.

'I'm going up there,' Farrow told Keesing. 'You can shout to me if you want me.'

Farrow climbed up the leg of the sitting man and sat down on the large rock. De Fries climbed up the gully and started to search for the entrance to the tomb. Keesing took torches and spades[43] out of the lorry and waited. After some time de Fries shouted down to Keesing, 'I've found some steps cut into the rock of the mountain!'

Keesing climbed up, carrying a torch and a spade. He looked at the steps. An enormous[44] rock had fallen down onto the steps from the mountain above.

'Farrow's right,' de Fries said to Keesing. 'The entrance is blocked. It will take weeks to get that enormous rock out of the way.'

Keesing looked around carefully on each side of the rock and then above it.

'I wonder what's above the rock,' said Keesing. 'I can't see up there. We'll have to climb up round it.'

Farrow watched the two men climb further up the gully. They climbed round the side of the enormous rock and disappeared.

What can I do to stop them? Farrow asked himself. There must be something I can do.

But then he remembered Christine and the radio call. He could do nothing until Keesing spoke to Greer on the radio.

I've shown them the tomb, he thought. Perhaps they'll let us go now.

Suddenly de Fries appeared again. He climbed down the gully

and hurried to the lorry. Then he climbed up the gully once more. This time he was carrying a box of dynamite.

'Have you found something?' Farrow shouted.

'There's a hole in the mountain above the rock,' replied de Fries. 'It looks like another way into the tomb.'

Farrow sat and waited. The sun had gone behind the mountain in the west. About fifteen minutes later, there was a loud explosion. Then silence.

Suddenly there was a loud scream. De Fries appeared at the top of the rock. But this time he did not climb down. He fell from the rock and rolled over and over into the valley below. He lay on the hard ground, his body turning and twisting. Then he gave another loud scream and lay still. Farrow knew that he was dead.

Farrow sat on the rock. De Fries was dead and there was nothing he could do for him. But where was Keesing? If Keesing was dead, no radio message would be sent to Greer and Christine would die.

Farrow climbed down and ran towards the gully. Suddenly he stopped. He had heard the sound of an engine. Farrow looked along the valley and saw a huge lorry coming towards him. The lorry stopped. Farrow watched in amazement. Three figures dressed in protective suits[45] climbed out of the lorry.

One of the figures moved towards Farrow. It stopped when it saw the body of de Fries. The man looked at Farrow and said, 'Who are you?'

'Farrow – Dr John Farrow. They made me take them here. They made me show them the tomb. Who are you? The police?'

'No, we're not the police. We've been following you. Thank you for writing such a clever book and for bringing us here. Let me introduce myself. My name is Strengel – Dr Jusef Strengel.'

One of the figures moved towards Farrow. It stopped when it saw the body of de Fries.

11

'We've Come Prepared'

Farrow had heard about Dr Strengel. He knew that Strengel was a rich man and owned a large collection of Egyptian antiquities.

Strengel pointed down at the body of de Fries.

'What's been happening here?' he asked.

'Keesing and de Fries blew open a passage into the Queen's tomb,' replied Farrow.

'Yes, we heard the explosion. It helped us to get here more quickly. Where's Keesing?'

'He's still in the tomb,' said Farrow. 'He's probably dead.'

'I found your book very helpful,' Dr Strengel told Farrow. 'I'm not a fool like Keesing. We've come prepared. No germs can get through these suits. Now we can take the mummy and treasure away before Inspector Salahadin arrives.'

Suddenly another voice interrupted them. It was Keesing. He had come out of the tomb while they had been talking. Now he was behind a rock. He was pointing a revolver at Strengel.

'You're not going to take the mummy or the treasure out of this tomb, Strengel,' said Keesing. 'I'm going to stop you.'

'Don't be a fool, Keesing,' said Strengel. 'You've been inside that tomb. The germs are in your body. You'll soon be dead like your friend, de Fries.'

'It was de Fries who was the fool,' replied Keesing. 'I didn't touch the mummy. It was de Fries who opened the case. I didn't touch it.'

'You've been in the tomb – that's enough,' said Strengel. 'You need help. I've got medicines in my lorry and I'm a doctor. Come down and I'll help you.'

There was a loud bang. A bullet from Keesing's revolver hit a

rock near Strengel.

'That suit won't protect you if it's got a hole in it,' shouted Keesing, with a laugh.

Suddenly there was another shot from behind Keesing. The revolver dropped from Keesing's hand. Keesing fell slowly from behind the rock. He rolled down the gully towards them. The driver of Strengel's lorry had crept up the rocks behind Keesing. The driver was not wearing a suit.

'Keep away from here!' Strengel shouted to the driver. 'Go and get your suit on. It's dangerous here.'

Farrow remembered that he was in danger too. He moved away from the bodies lying on the rocks. Strengel looked down at Keesing. Keesing was not dead, but his face was turning black. He was in great pain.

'Shoot me – shoot me,' he said to Strengel. 'You were right. The germs are in my body. Shoot me now. Let me die quickly.'

51

'You knew that you were dying. And you wanted me to die in the same way,' was Strengel's cruel reply. He walked away, leaving Keesing turning and twisting in great pain.

Strengel turned to the two men who were with him, 'We can go into the tomb now and get the mummy. But we must be quick.'

'What about the radio message?' said Farrow, turning to Dr Strengel.

'What radio message?'

'They're holding my wife prisoner in Cairo,' Farrow explained. 'If Greer doesn't get a call from Keesing before seven o'clock, he'll kill my wife. And it's nearly seven o'clock now.'

'I haven't got time for that,' replied Strengel cruelly. He walked back to his lorry to get the equipment ready. They had powerful lights, spades, ropes, and steel bars. Strengel and his three men climbed up the gully. They were all wearing their protective suits.

Farrow stood thinking for a few moments. Then he walked down towards the lorry. He would try to use the radio to speak to Greer. He had never used a radio before, but he had watched Keesing using it.

———

In the Range Rover, Salahadin had also heard the explosion.

'That's them,' he said. 'They're near.'

'The explosion was on the other side of that mountain,' said the driver. 'It won't be easy to get there.'

'Which mountain?' asked Musa.

The driver pointed up to a mountain top to the east.

'That's the mountain shaped like a sitting man,' he said. 'We'll have to get round to the other side of that mountain.'

'Let's get there as quickly as we can then,' said Salahadin. 'The sun's setting now and it will soon be dark.'

'It'll be dangerous if we drive too quickly,' said the driver.

'Drive as quickly as you can,' Salahadin repeated. 'If they take that mummy out of the tomb, it could be much more dangerous for everyone.'

The driver drove the Range Rover round rocks and up over hills of sand. The passengers were thrown from one side to the other. Half an hour later, they reached the entrance to the valley. The driver stopped.

'We must be very near now,' he said to Salahadin. 'I've been in this valley before. There's a gully on the west side. It's below that great rock on top. The tomb must be in the gully.'

'Good,' said Salahadin. 'We can walk from here.'

They all got out of the Range Rover. The driver pointed to some tyre marks in the sand.

'We'll follow these tracks,' said Salahadin quietly.

They walked slowly down the valley. Salahadin and Musa went in front, with their revolvers ready. The three policemen and the driver followed them. They found the two lorries standing in the valley.

'Listen,' whispered Salahadin.

They stood and listened. A noise came from the back of one of the lorries.

'It's someone tuning[46] a radio,' said the driver. 'I used to work as a radio operator. I'd know that noise anywhere.'

Salahadin walked up to the back of the lorry and looked inside. Someone was sitting in front of a radio with his back towards Salahadin.

'Put your hands up and turn round,' Salahadin said quietly.

Farrow was startled and jumped up and turned round. Salahadin was ready to shoot if the man had a gun. But he recognised Farrow immediately. He had seen his photograph on the visa application form in London.

'You're Farrow – Dr John Farrow,' said Salahadin. 'What's going on here? Where are the others?'

'Who are you?' asked Farrow.

'I'm Salahadin El Nur – a police officer.'

'Thank goodness you've come at last,' said Farrow.

Farrow quickly told Salahadin about the deaths of de Fries and Keesing, and about Strengel and his men.

'Where's Strengel now?' Salahadin asked.

Farrow started to explain about the danger in the tomb. Salahadin stopped him.

'I've read your book and I know all about that. Tell me about Strengel and his men.'

'They're in the tomb,' replied Farrow. 'But they're wearing protective suits, and they're protected from the germs. They're taking the mummy out – '

'They're not leaving here,' said Salahadin. 'The Queen of Death must stay in her tomb forever.'

'But how are you going to stop them?'

'I've got men with me,' was Salahadin's reply.

Farrow then told Salahadin about the radio call to Greer.

'I'll send the driver in to you,' replied Salahadin. 'He knows about radios.'

Salahadin hurried back to the others and told them what was happening. He pointed to the enormous rock that had fallen over the entrance to the tomb.

'They've found a way into the tomb above that rock,' he said. 'They're going to carry the mummy down the gully. They're wearing protective suits and they won't be able to move easily. That's where we'll be able to stop them.'

Salahadin then reminded them of the dangers of going too near the mummy.

'Don't go near the mummy,' he said. 'Remember – if you touch the mummy, you will die a horrible death.'

Salahadin turned to the driver.

'Go back to the lorry and help Farrow send a radio message,' he said. 'But do it cleverly. If the person in Cairo gets suspicious, he may kill Christine Farrow.'

Salahadin sent two of the policemen up one side of the gully. The third policeman climbed up the other side.

The policemen quietly took up their places and hid behind rocks. Musa climbed above the entrance to the tomb and stood in the shadow of a rock. The moon shone on Salahadin who was standing alone in the gully.

12

The Radio Call

Inside the lorry, the driver looked quickly through the pieces of paper beside the radio. He found notes made by Keesing. They were notes for his calls to Greer in Cairo.

'It won't take long now,' he explained to Farrow. 'I'm going to call Greer in Cairo. When Greer replies, I'll cut off the power[47]. He'll think that Keesing is trying to get through to him. He'll go on trying to speak to us. We'll pretend that we're trying to speak to him. That will keep him busy.'

The driver tuned in the radio and gave the call sign[48]. A few moments later, Greer replied. The driver immediately cut off the power and counted twenty. Then he switched the power on again and repeated the call sign.

Back in Cairo, Greer answered the call sign three times. But all he got back in reply was the call sign.

There's something wrong with their radio, he thought. I'll have to keep on trying.

By now Leila was inside the house. She followed Fatima's instructions and made her way to the man's bedroom. She stood outside the door and listened. She heard the man using a radio transmitter.

He's busy with a radio in there, she thought. That gives me time to find the woman.

She again followed Fatima's instructions and went to the locked door of the woman's bedroom. She stood listening, but there was no sound. She tapped the door lightly with her fingers and waited. There was no reply. She tapped the door again, this time a little louder. She heard the noise of someone moving.

'Who is it? What do you want?' said a voice on the other side of the locked door.

'I thought I heard someone crying,' said Leila. 'Are you all right?'

'Who are you?'

'I'm the servant,' replied Leila. 'Are you all right?'

'Can you take a message for me?' asked the voice.

'A message for your husband?' said Leila.

'No – no – that man's not my husband,' said the voice. 'Don't tell him you've spoken to me . . .'

'Who are you?' Leila asked quietly.

'My name is Farrow – Christine Farrow. Can you take a message to the police?'

'It's all right, Mrs Farrow,' said Leila. 'I am a police officer. Stay where you are. We'll soon have you out of there.'

'Take care,' whispered Christine Farrow. 'The man's very dangerous and he's got a gun.'

'We'll take care,' answered Leila. 'You wait there quietly.'

Leila went back towards the front door. Suddenly she heard the door of the man's bedroom opening. It was Greer coming out of his bedroom. He had remembered that the servant was still in the house.

Greer stood outside his bedroom door and turned to lock it behind him. Just as he was turning the key, he heard the call sign again. He stood with the key in his hand.

'OK – OK, I'm coming,' he said and opened the door again and went back to the radio.

13

Salahadin's Bluff

Half-way up the gully, Salahadin stood waiting in the moon-light. Musa and the policemen were hidden behind rocks.

At last Salahadin heard the noise he was waiting for. Strengel and his men were carrying the mummy out of the tomb. He waited patiently until Strengel came round the rock. Strengel did not notice him. He had his back towards Salahadin and was giving instructions to his men.

'Carefully now – go carefully,' said Strengel to the men above him.

A few moments later, Strengel turned round to look for a path down the gully. He saw Salahadin standing below him.

'Salahadin El Nur,' said Strengel. 'I didn't expect you so soon. Have you come here to help us?'

'I've come to help you put the mummy back in the tomb,' replied Salahadin quietly.

'I'm taking the mummy away with me,' said Strengel. 'And you won't be able to stop me.'

'I've got my men all round you,' said Salahadin. 'And they've got orders to shoot.'

'Order them to shoot if you want,' said Strengel. 'But think what will happen before you give the order. Remember you haven't got protective suits. I was the one clever enough to think of suits to protect us from the germs. Without these suits, you cannot come near the mummy. If you shoot us, we'll drop the mummy. It will break open if it falls and the germs will spread everywhere.'

Salahadin stood looking up at Strengel. For a few seconds, there was a strange silence in the moonlit gully.

'I've told my men to shoot you in the legs,' said Salahadin. 'A space suit with holes in it will not protect you.'

'And my orders to my men are to drop the mummy if I am shot,' replied Strengel. 'We are coming down now.'

Strengel's men began to move. Strengel's men carefully lowered the mummy down over the large rock. Strengel came nearer to Salahadin.

'You'd better move,' advised Strengel.

Salahadin waited until Strengel was a few metres away. Then he raised his revolver.

'Stop where you are,' he said to Strengel. 'Stop or I shoot.'

'Shoot me and you'll die – and your policemen with you,' replied Strengel.

'You're all going to die anyway,' shouted Salahadin loudly. He wanted Strengel's men to hear him. 'Didn't Farrow tell you about the acid[49]?'

Strengel stood still and his men stopped moving.

'What acid?' asked Strengel.

'There's a strong acid on the walls of the tomb and on the mummy,' replied Salahadin. 'The acid is slowly burning through your suits and through your gloves. When it has burnt through, the germs of the disease will follow it. Then you will all die like de Fries and Keesing.'

Strengel's men looked at one another carefully. Then they lowered the mummy down onto the ground below the rock. They looked at their gloves and at their space suits.

'He's bluffing[50],' shouted Strengel, turning back to face them. 'It isn't true. There isn't any acid that can last for thousands of years. It's a bluff.'

But his men did not move. They were not sure if Salahadin was speaking the truth.

'You'll soon feel the acid burning your hands,' Salahadin shouted up at them. 'Then it will be too late. The germs will be inside your suits.'

Suddenly one of Strengel's men began to tear off the gloves of his suit. He believed what Salahadin was saying. The sweat caused by the rubber gloves was making his hands itch[51].

'I can feel my hands burning!' he shouted. 'I'm getting out of this suit before the germs kill me.'

'You fool,' shouted Strengel. 'You're sure to die now. Your suit is covered with germs.'

Strengel was right. As the man was pulling the suit off from his legs, he gave a loud scream. He rolled forward and fell down the gully, turning and twisting. Salahadin jumped to one side. The man rolled past him and lay twisting in pain beside the dead body of Keesing.

Strengel suddenly ran towards Salahadin. He wanted to touch Salahadin with the outside of his suit. Salahadin would die too. But Strengel could not move quickly because of the suit. Salahadin shot Strengel in the leg. Strengel screamed with pain and fell to the ground.

Salahadin shouted to Musa and the policemen.

'Come out now,' he said. 'Watch these men.'

Then he looked up and spoke to Strengel's men.

'The acid will take some time to burn through,' he told them. 'Before it does, you have time to carry the mummy back into the tomb. Then we'll help you to take those suits off carefully.'

Strengel's men did not know what to do. The man lying beside Keesing gave a loud scream and died.

'You haven't got much time,' Salahadin shouted. 'Get that mummy back into the tomb quickly. It's your only hope of staying alive.'

The men carefully lifted up the mummy and began to move it back into the tomb. Inspector Musa climbed down towards them.

'Keep back – keep away from them, Musa,' shouted Salahadin.

Salahadin told one of the policemen to go back to the Range Rover, 'Bring me the box of dynamite,' he said. 'I am going to shut the Queen of Death in her tomb forever.'

———

Back in Cairo, Leila opened the front door of the house. Inspector Ahmed was waiting outside with the two policemen.

'Christine Farrow is locked in one bedroom,' said Leila quickly. 'The man's in another room – he's using a radio.'

'Let's get him first,' said Ahmed. 'Show me the way.'

Ahmed and the two policemen followed Leila. Leila pointed to a bedroom door.

'He's in there,' said Leila.

Ahmed walked quietly up to the bedroom door. He turned the handle, but the door was locked. Ahmed stood back with his revolver in his hand. One of the policemen crashed against the door with his shoulder. The door broke open and they ran into the room.

'Police – the police are here,' shouted Greer into the radio.

Ahmed pointed his revolver at Greer, 'You're under arrest[52],' he said. 'Give me the keys to the other bedroom.'

Suddenly a voice came from the radio. It was the voice of Dr Farrow.

'What's happening there?' asked Farrow. 'What did you say about the police?'

Ahmed went over to the radio. 'Who's calling?' he asked.

Farrow explained who he was and where he was calling from.

'What about Inspector Salahadin?' asked Ahmed.

'He's here,' said Farrow. 'What about my wife?'

'Your wife is all right,' said Ahmed. 'What's happening where you are?'

Farrow began to explain, but he was stopped by the voice of Salahadin.

'This is Inspector Salahadin El Nur. Who's that?'

'It's Inspector Ahmed speaking. Hello, Salahadin. Everything's all right here. Christine Farrow is safe and well. How are you?'

'We've got to move out of here quickly,' replied Salahadin. 'I've put dynamite under a rock at the top of a mountain. The dynamite is going to explode in a few minutes. Keep listening – you'll hear the noise.'

The policemen took Greer away. Ahmed sat down near the radio, and Leila brought Christine Farrow into the room. She was crying.

'You can stop worrying. Your husband is safe,' Inspector Ahmed told her. 'I've just spoken to him on the radio. Everything is all right.'

14

The Tomb is Sealed

The two lorries were driven back up the valley. Salahadin switched on the radio again and called Ahmed.

'Get ready for the noise of the explosion,' he told Ahmed. 'We're going to take shelter.'

Salahadin got out of the lorry and went with Musa and Dr Farrow behind some rocks.

The policemen and the rest of Strengel's men went behind rocks too.

A few seconds later, there was a loud explosion. The head of the man on top of the mountain began to break into pieces. The pieces fell down into the gully. Soon the gully was completely filled with enormous rocks.

Salahadin and the others came out from behind the rocks.

A few seconds later, there was a loud explosion.

'We'll have to stay here until the sun comes up again,' Salahadin said to Musa. 'We must make sure that everything is completely covered over.'

Ahmed's voice came from the radio in the lorry.

'Salahadin, are you all right? Are you all right?'

Salahadin turned to Dr Farrow.

'You can answer that question,' he said to Farrow. 'And you can say hello to your wife.'

Farrow went towards the lorry. Musa shouted after him.

'Thanks for telling Salahadin about the acid,' he said. 'That saved all our lives.'

'Acid?' said Farrow. 'What acid – I don't know what you're talking about.'

Farrow hurried to the lorry. Musa turned to Salahadin who was laughing quietly.

'I tricked you too,' said Salahadin. 'Let's get some blankets. It's been a long day and I need some sleep.'

POINTS
FOR
UNDERSTANDING

Points for Understanding

1

1 Why was Salahadin able to go on holiday in August?
2 What subject did Leila and Salahadin study at Cairo University?
3 In a bookshop in Piccadilly, Salahadin noticed a book which interested him.
    (a) What was the title of the book?
    (b) What was the name of the author?
    (c) What was unusual about the author's name?

2

1 Dr Peter Earl showed Salahadin a news item in *The Sunday Times*. The item was about a young archeologist.
    (a) What was the archeologist's name?
    (b) What did the archeologist believe about some writings on a pillar from the Temple of Karnak?
    (c) Where did the news item say the archeologist was going?
    (d) What was he going to do there?
2 Who else knew about the writings on the pillar from the Temple of Karnak?
3 What was the Amsterdam Ring?
4 Why was Salahadin going to be arriving late at the British Museum on the following morning?

3

1 Where did Inspector Ahmed say the Farrows were?
2 Salahadin noticed two unusual things about John Farrow's application for an Egyptian visa. What were they?
3 Salahadin had two things to do in London before he flew back to Cairo. What were they?
4 What was unusual about the news item in *The Sunday Times*?
5 Where had John Farrow gone after he left Cambridge University?

6 Salahadin asked Peter Earl: 'Do you believe that Farrow has discovered the burial place of Queen Axtarte?' What was Peter Earl's reply?
7 Who had told *The Sunday Times* about Farrow's visit to Egypt?

4

1 Why did Salahadin ask Inspector Ahmed if he had looked for Farrow in Luxor?
2 Why was Queen Axtarte buried on the east bank of the Nile?
3 Who did Salahadin think was with Dr Farrow?
4 Why did Salahadin ask the driver to stop at a cigarette kiosk?
5 What two things did Salahadin find in the black Mercedes? Why were they important?

5

1 There was a feast after the burial of Queen Axtarte. What happened to the nobles who attended the feast?
2 What did one of the mourners manage to do before he died?
3 Salahadin asked Professor Gomouchian: 'If you found the Queen's tomb, would you go into it and touch anything?' What was the professor's reply?
4 'I think we've found something,' Leila said to Ahmed.
   (a) Where was Leila standing?
   (b) What did she see among the rubbish?

6

1 Farrow had left a message.
   (a) Where had he left it?
   (b) Who was holding him prisoner?
   (c) Where were they taking him?
   (d) What was happening to his wife?
   (e) Who did Farrow want the message to be passed to?
2 Where in Cairo did Salahadin say the gang might be holding Mrs Farrow prisoner?
3 Why would it be very dangerous if the Amsterdam Ring took anything out of the Queen's tomb?

7

1 How long had Farrow been in the desert with Keesing and de Fries?
2 What was Keesing going to do if Farrow did not take them to the tomb by seven o'clock?
3 What was Farrow going to do when he took them to the tomb?
4 Why did Keesing not want the lorry to go up over the hill?

8

1 Why did the pilot not think the two lorries in the desert were travelling together?
2 How had Ahmed found out that Dr Jusef Strengel was in Egypt?
3 'We know a lot about Dr Strengel,' Salahadin told Inspector Musa Angheli. Why was Dr Strengel different from other smugglers of antiquities?
4 Who did Salahadin think was in the first lorry and in the second lorry?
5 Salahadin took something unusual with them in the Range Rover. What was it?

9

1 Why were the other servants interested in the people Fatima worked for?
2 Ahmed asked Fatima: 'How do you know it's a woman in the bedroom?'
    (a) How did Fatima know?
    (b) How long had the woman been there?
3 What was Fatima on her way to buy?
4 What did Leila plan to do when she got into the house where Fatima worked?
5 What did Ahmed think of Leila's plan?

10

1 How did Farrow know that they had reached the valley where the Queen's tomb was?
2 Where did Farrow say the tomb was in the valley?

3 Why could it often take a long time to get inside a tomb?
4 Why could Farrow not go very far away from Keesing?
5 Suddenly there was a loud explosion.
    (a) How was Keesing trying to get into the tomb?
    (b) What happened to de Fries shortly after the explosion?
6 Who had followed Farrow to the Queen's tomb?

11

1 Dr Strengel told Farrow: 'We've come prepared.' How had Dr Strengel come prepared?
2 Why did Keesing ask Strengel to kill him with a shot from his gun?
3 Why did the Range Rover driver know that someone was operating a radio in the lorry?

12

1 How was the driver tricking Greer on the radio?
2 Who was the woman in the bedroom?
3 Greer was coming out of the bedroom to speak to the servant. Why did he change his mind and go back into his bedroom?

13

1 Where had Salahadin ordered the policemen to shoot Strengel and his men?
2 What orders had Strengel given to his men if they were shot?
3 What did Salahadin tell Strengel's men which made them afraid?
4 'Bring the box of dynamite,' Salahadin told a policeman. What was Salahadin planning to do?
5 How did Farrow learn that the police had captured Greer?

14

1 Why did Salahadin have to wait near the valley until sunrise?
2 'I tricked you too,' Salahadin said to Musa Angheli. How had Salahadin tricked Strengel's men?

GLOSSARY

Glossary

1 *attract* (page 5)

if something attracts you, you want to go to it. Thieves went to the tombs looking for treasure.

2 *smuggle* (page 5)

there are many things which cannot be taken out of or brought into a country without permission, or without paying money. To smuggle something out of a country is to take the thing out without permission.

3 *customs and immigration officials* (page 8)

these officials work at airports and seaports. The custom officials try to stop people smuggling goods into or out of the country. The immigration officials check the passports of people coming into or leaving a country.

4 *suburb* (page 9)

a part of a city away from the centre.

5 *ancestors* (page 10)

the Ancient Egyptians are the forefathers – the ancestors – of many of the people who live in Egypt today.

6 *scholar* (page 12)

someone who studies a subject very deeply.

7 *telex* (page 12)

a typed message sent like a telephone message from one place to another – often from one country to another. A telex is received as quickly as a telephone call.

8 *Ministry of the Interior* (page 12)

the government department in a country which looks after the police and is responsible for the laws is often called the Ministry of the Interior.

9 *Visa Section* (page 14)

a visa is permission to enter a country or to leave it. The visa is stamped on your passport and checked by the immigration officials. The Visa Section is the department of an Embassy or Consulate where you go to get a visa.

10 *confirmed* (page 14)

if you think something is wrong or unusual, you become suspicious. If you then learn that you are correct and that something is wrong, your suspicions are confirmed.

11 *deceive* (page 18)
to tell lies to someone is to deceive them.

12 *drugs* (page 18)
something which you eat or smoke or put into your body which changes the way you feel, e.g. cannabis or hashish, cocaine, etc. Some drugs, like tobacco, are permitted. Other drugs, like cannabis, are not permitted in most countries.

13 *involved* (page 18)
to be involved with someone is to be working with them – often when they are doing something wrong.

14 *roundabout* (page 21)
a large circle built at a road junction where many roads meet. The traffic – cars and lorries and buses – have to go slowly round the roundabout before turning off on the road they are going.

15 *kiosk* (page 21)
a small shop at the side of the road. Cigarettes and newspapers are often sold at kiosks.

16 *foreign number plate* (page 21)
the number plate on a car shows the country the car is registered in – usually where the owner of the car lives. The number plate on the black Mercedes was foreign – it was not Egyptian.

17 *tram* (page 22)
transport in a city which runs along the streets on rails and is driven by electricity. See the illustration on page 23.

18 *accelerator* (page 22)
the pedal which the driver of a car presses with his foot to make the car go faster.

19 *squeal* (page 22)
if you brake a car suddenly, the brakes often make a loud, sharp sound. The brakes squeal.

20 *traffic policeman* (page 22)
a policeman whose job is to control traffic on the city streets.

21 *identity card* (page 22)
a card which a policeman carries to show that he is a policeman. The card has the policeman's photograph fixed to it and his name and number written on it.

22 *tow* (page 24)
to tie a rope to a car and pull it along behind another car or lorry.

23 *statue* (page 24)

a statue is made of stone, metal or wood and shaped like a person or an animal.

24 *wheelchair* (page 25)

Professor Gomouchian cannot walk and he sits in a chair which has wheels. He can move the chair round the room. He has a rug – a piece of cloth made of wool – over his legs to keep them warm.

25 *slaves* (page 25)

slaves were owned by their masters and had to do what their masters told them. They worked hard and were given food and clothing, but they were not given money.

26 *nobles* (page 25)

rich and important people who are given power by the king or queen of a country.

27 *poison* (page 26)

to poison food or drink is to put something in the food or drink which will kill anyone who eats or drinks it.

28 *mourners* (page 26)

someone who goes to the funeral of a dead person.

29 *diseases* (page 26)

dangerous illnesses. When a person is affected by the germs of a disease, they become ill and often they die. When many people in a country all have the same disease and many are dying, the disease is called a plague.

30 *hotel register* (page 27)

a book in a hotel where everyone who stays in the hotel must write down his name and home address.

31 *pretend* (page 32)

to say something which you know is not true.

32 *powerful radio transmitter* (page 32)

a strong radio which sends and receives messages to and from places which are far from each other.

33 *to get rid of* (page 32)

to kill someone. A way of speaking used by criminals.

34 *compass* (page 34)

the pointer in a compass always points to the North. A traveller in the desert uses a compass to show the direction he wants to go.

35 **dizzy** (page 34)
when you feel dizzy, you feel strange and uncomfortable. When you feel dizzy, you have to sit or lie down. The strong heat of the sun made Dr Farrow feel dizzy.

36 **binoculars** (page 36)
you look through binoculars with both eyes and are able to see clearly things which are far away. See the illustration on page 37.

37 **desert tracks** (page 39)
rough paths going across a desert.

38 **rifles** (page 39)
the policemen are carrying rifles – large guns which can shoot over long distances. Salahadin and Musa carry *revolvers* – small hand guns.

39 **dynamite** (page 39)
a powerful explosive. When dynamite explodes, it can break large rocks into small pieces.

40 **cautiously** (page 43)
very slowly and carefully.

41 **gully** (page 46)
where a stream has cut into a mountainside many years before and left a narrow, steep passage.

42 **blast** (page 46)
to explode dynamite so that it breaks into small pieces any large rock which is sealing the entrance to the tomb.

43 **torches and spades** (page 47)
Keesing and de Fries need torches to give them light inside the dark tomb. And they need spades to dig away earth and stones.

44 **enormous** (page 47)
very, very large.

45 **protective suits** (page 48)
special clothing to keep a person who wears it safe. See the illustration on page 49.

46 **tune a radio** (page 53)
to turn the controls of a radio so that you can hear the message clearly. The radio operator is someone who knows how to use a radio and to tune it correctly.

47 **power** (page 55)
the electricity which makes a radio work.

48 *call sign* (page 55)
   at the beginning of a radio message, the operator sends a signal to tell
   the listener who he is and who he wants to speak to.
49 *acid* (page 59)
   a liquid which burns through rubber or cloth. If you get acid on your
   hands, it will burn your skin.
50 *bluff* (page 60)
   a bluff is when you trick someone by telling them something which is
   not true.
51 *itch* (page 60)
   when your skin itches, you want to scratch it with your fingers.
52 *under arrest* (page 62)
   when a policeman takes someone prisoner, he must warn the prisoner
   and say: 'You are under arrest.' Then the policeman can take his
   prisoner to the police station.

Shane *by Jack Schaefer*
Old Mali and the Boy *by D. R. Sherman*
Bristol Murder *by Philip Prowse*
Tales of Goha *by Leslie Caplan*
The Smuggler *by Piers Plowright*
The Pearl *by John Steinbeck*
Things Fall Apart *by Chinua Achebe*
The Woman Who Disappeared *by Philip Prowse*
The Moon is Down *by John Steinbeck*
A Town Like Alice *by Nevil Shute*
The Queen of Death *by John Milne*
Walkabout *by James Vance Marshall*
Meet Me in Istanbul *by Richard Chisholm*
The Great Gatsby *by F. Scott Fitzgerald*
The Space Invaders *by Geoffrey Matthews*
My Cousin Rachel *by Daphne du Maurier*
I'm the King of the Castle *by Susan Hill*
Dracula *by Bram Stoker*
The Sign of Four *by Sir Arthur Conan Doyle*
The Speckled Band and Other Stories *by Sir Arthur Conan Doyle*
The Eye of the Tiger *by Wilbur Smith*
The Queen of Spades and Other Stories *by Aleksandr Pushkin*
The Diamond Hunters *by Wilbur Smith*
When Rain Clouds Gather *by Bessie Head*
Banker *by Dick Francis*
No Longer at Ease *by Chinua Achebe*
The Franchise Affair *by Josephine Tey*
The Case of the Lonely Lady *by John Milne*

For further information on the full selection of
Readers at all five levels in the series, please refer
to the Heinemann Guided Readers catalogue.

Heinemann English Language Teaching
A division of Heinemann Publishers (Oxford) Ltd
Halley Court, Jordan Hill, Oxford OX2 8EJ

OXFORD MADRID ATHENS PARIS FLORENCE PRAGUE
SÃO PAULO CHICAGO MELBOURNE AUCKLAND
SINGAPORE TOKYO GABORONE
JOHANNESBURG PORTSMOUTH (NH) IBADAN

ISBN 0 435 27238 1

© John Milne 1979, 1992
First published 1979
Reprinted four times
This edition published 1992

Illustrated by Peter Dennis
Typography by Adrian Hodgkins
Cover by Jean-Christian Knaff and Threefold Design
Typeset in 11/12.5 pt Goudy
by Joshua Associates Ltd, Oxford
Printed and bound in Malta by Interprint Limited

94 95 96 97 10 9 8 7 6 5 4